NO GUARDIANS
for the
HALF-BROKEN

JONATHAN IAN ELLIOTT

ISBN: 978-1-960146-99-1

Elliott. Jonathan

Edited by: Barbara Henn and Amy Ashby

Warren
publishing

Published by Warren Publishing
Charlotte, NC
www.warrenpublishing.net
Printed in the United States

I dedicate this book of poetry to Barbara Henn.

Barbara was there for me from the first day when I returned to writing poetry after a nearly thirty-year layoff. As an educator, she was as encouraging as she was honest regarding the quality of my work. And in those early days, admittedly, the quality just wasn't always there, although I had published poetry in the early seventies in the Virginia Commonwealth University literary magazine as well as several times in a small magazine in New York that paid a small sum per poem and several copies each time.

Barbara has reviewed and edited give or take a thousand of the three thousand poems I've written in my most productive days in the Cornelius/Davidson, North Carolina area.

Yes, I wrote some bad poetry in those early days. But it was Pulitzer Prize winning poet Philip Levine in a lecture at the New York Writers Institute on February 4, 2015 who said, "We all learn to accept our failures .... Walt Whitman wrote badly. He's our greatest poet. Emily Dickinson wrote badly. She's damned near our greatest poet. If our greatest poets can write badly, we can write badly."

I leave it up to my readers of *No Guardians for the Half-Broken* to determine if I've provided them with quality verse.

AUTHOR'S NOTE

Recently, a physician diagnosed me with PTSD at seventy-five years old and has recommended a specific therapy for that condition. That's after ten years of therapy from my early twenties to early thirties, more than forty years later. Often, I still have trouble sleeping at night.

While my father never saw a therapist and therefore was never diagnosed with PTSD, it seems almost certain we suffered from the same condition. We have been, indeed, among the half-broken. While I have no knowledge of the condition that sent her there, my West Virginia grandmother went into therapy when she was in her sixties.

OF RAGE
and
BEAUTY

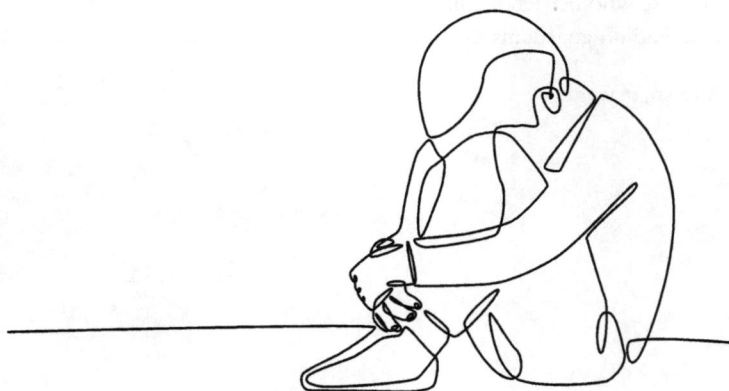

No Guardians for the Half-Broken

There were no guardians for the half-broken.
At war's end, unraveling what civilian life imposed,

the young sailor relied on his mother for forgiveness
of images and dreams, the real, the imaginary ones.

Warfare was like that. The longing for friends who vowed
to salvage what was left of him. The salve they gave
to try and bring him back to who he'd been.

There was no what was. No re-dos.
Time made no mends, nor amends.

Just rage left as residue.
The sway of the nights that faded
into the morning light. The innocence
of those who befriended him. Those
who had no guardians themselves.

And so, it went.

Crimson Roses and Purple Irises

I am the son
      of a sixteen-year-old girl who married to escape
   what seemed like poverty to her then,

only to discover
      her poverty was a name her married man used
   to break her down,

again, again. He came from good folks, he said.
      I was the outsider at home to him, save
   my skin most seasoned to a belt buckle slash.

"If you fall, or whine, we will start again," this man
      called father said.

"Never tell anyone what goes on in this house!"
my mother often screamed.

As I grow older, the memory
of those words is as powerful as
   the belt slashes themselves.

I call the blood on my legs back then my crimson roses,
      and the purple and yellow bruises my irises—
   my mother's favorite flower.

      And as I've made peace with all this, I call it poetry.

The Eyes of a Drowsy Owl,
The Gray Sway of Sycamore Shadows

For a moment, the eyes
of a drowsy owl nearly
        camouflaged on a poplar tree

eased the recall, the sting of flesh,
        the quick white crack of a back hand.

There were no Jesuses to protect
            a boy from this, only a run to the woods
        where the bloom of hope rose

from the sun on the river, the gray sway
        of sycamore shadows and boughs of pines
    displaying what godliness was.

The air drenched in solitude, the rush of a frenetic
        heart submerged into the slow calm
    away from the ungodly. The threads of pain and
        beauty wove into
    a boy becoming who he was.

A boy becomes a man so quickly, it is only
        near the end he understands.

A man called father left the earth with
        his sorrows, regrets.

"I can't sleep at night, thinking
        what I did to you back then," the man
    called father once said.

"It's okay," the boy turned man said.

There is forgiveness in recalling the drowsy eyes
        of an owl, the bloom of hope that rose
    from the sun on the river,

the gray sway of sycamore shadows and
boughs of pines displaying what godliness is.

For all that, it's what makes
        up the sweet nature of poetry
    in all its pain and beauty.

When One Crack of the Backhand
Wasn't Enough
(Or, That's Just the Way Life Was)

When the man called father struck the boy
to the fuse of skin and nerve, the lad bled so
easily, a face the shade of crimson red.

The child bore neither fear nor rage,
just another disheartening, in shame,
dishonoring of who he thought he was.

The hint of blood, nose to nostril flowed;
 the tongue tastes what it does.

That's just the way life was.

The pain, fathoms deep that marred
the core of who he was before the boy
was ten. So deep there's no escape
from who he'd become.

The splitting of an eyelid, half-blind,
the boy dared not blink.

That's just the way life was.

What does it take for a man to bruise
the flesh of those he says, at times,
he loves? Who beats them till the rage
subsides,

the weighty cadence of that crack
that drives the will of that man, and
a child left dreamless inside?

No death occurs more natural than this.

That's just the way life was.

And in the end the images remain.
The boy turned man offsets those unruly days
with sounds of violins and music so soft
sometimes he weeps for what might have been,
unlike the way life was.

Of Rage and Beauty

The man called father recoils. The salvo
of mouth's blood, that taste, will stop soon.

Everything will be alright, the boy is schooled
to believe. But it is a rewind of the reel to recall
where blood roses grow. His back. His legs.

"You will never touch that boy again!" the mother says.
It is a story told, again and again. It is one of a dozen
times they will leave this man for the blue-green scent
of mountains, train rides away.

The force that pulses through the flesh searches for solitude.
It is what makes the unfaithful faithful knowing the pain will really
end. To survive stirs the slightest triumph of boy over man.

The bandage is silence. Quiet. Peace. It is what
the boy chooses to perceive after all this. In the absence
of perfection, beyond the right hand of rage, beauty endures
among the simplest of things.

A creek where minnows thrive. To run his fingers against
the current's flow. To know this is what life really is.

Ghost-Child and Woman
with the Raccoon Eyes

When the man called father came,
Mom screamed, "I'll never go back with you!
"Get in the goddam car!" He wrenched her

by the arm. She, with her raccoon eyes,
bruised cheeks, stared back at me.
"Where are they going?" I asked, but no

one answered. "Are they coming back?"
Again, the words drifted about as though
never spoken to a ghost-child.

The
STRENGTH
of
MOUNTAIN
WOMEN

What the Strength of a Woman Means

I never knew my grandfathers. One
died before my birth. The other left
my grandmother seven kids to feed.

I learned the strength of the womenfolk
early in pre-teens. One, a nurse, spent days
tossing her patients about, changed

their sheets, wiped them clean. She saved
her money to own property she rented out
to church folks she knew. She lent money

to my mother when my father binged,
who drank bourbon even when the street lights
dwindled into dawn, and morning

brought the rooster out to send him
off to bed. My mother clerked at the Five
and Dime to pay his debts.

Grandma Tucker spent her time
washing, ironing clothes for neighbors
who paid her by the day, a few dollars

and change. She only alluded once
to the ghost of the man who left her
for his Southern *hussy*. It was what

life was, and that was the end of it.
Her women-children set out from home
in their teens. Sent cash back to pay

for their mother's partial teeth & linen
clothes. She drew from her garden
the rest of her needs, save the price

of coal in freezing seasons. There always
seemed to be just enough to pay for a dump
truck full, emptied on the side of the house.

I never saw these women fear much of anything.
They seemed to believe that fear had no regard
for whether they acknowledged it or not.

A Certain Strength

It takes a certain strength to live in poverty where
the sun towers over a thousand mountain villages,

and countless stars are the greatest light over what
darkness brings. Fertile valleys and a hundred rivers

give common folks land for farms, streams to cast
a line, the ransom of the land to survive. The joy

of hypnotic voices, toe-tapping with their fiddles
and autoharps, tell the story of a hundred years

or more of plights and give light to all that is celestial,
these people of the bright moon and solitude of hills.

Among the hollowed glens of autumn, they sing
of harvest and what it means when winter comes.

Give thanks to the splendor of summer seeds.
They are enamored by the hills they may see

as temples when others may think of them
as tethered birds. If the meek shall inherit

the earth, heaven is theirs among the fields of corn,
peach trees, and apples that grow endlessly. Near

penniless, it's just enough for them to carry on
as though life meant something more.

Only the Taste of Loneliness
(The Whitesville Mine Explosion, 2010)

New widows left motionless: what is there to say to gods
that never heard a prayer? Unwelcomed hours to digest

what happened here. Those stitched fray-collared shirts
she'd sworn she would replace come payday.

Despair, a lifetime to relive lunchpails sandwiched-up
with ham, homemade bread, and cheese. The tale that lingers

in what used to be those early morning hours. Old bedsheets,
her new beginnings, even as she sensed the scent of him.

There is still the beauty of the land—blue spruce trees,
creeks that run through nearly every vein of life surrounding

her, but for this grandeur-turned-grotesque for the lifeless
living. The laughter, that lost thing, that whiled away

the hours when mealtime came. Now only the taste,
the spoils, of loneliness remains.

Aunt Betty's House

I remember waking at Aunt Betty's
to watch the dew light up blades of grass,

crystals shining on sunlit grounds.
Barefoot I walked among the vanes of green.

The weak ones broke underfoot.
I shivered in the cool dew.

The mountain air closed in on me,
yet gave me a freedom I had rarely felt

when the distant hills rolled on endlessly.
The trees, a mass of bluish green,

rounded the bend where almost out of sight
the Petries lived.

I never wanted those times to end.
The sound of the hollow echoed my name

until the years finally passed me by.
At fifty, I visited the homestead again

where Aunt Betty had made the best cornbread,
where she would call me in—

"Breakfast, boy. We'll begin without you if you're late."
I looked inside the brindled, broken window now.

I was never late, save this time.
Save this time.

*Recipient, Honorable Mention for Emerging
Poets, 2017, West Virginia Writers Group*

*One of the few poems I had sent out for
publication or contest after a nearly forty year
layoff from poetry writing. I was sixty-nine when
winning Honorable Mention as an "Emerging Poet."*

In the Silence of Time

Middle-aged, a man walks down a dirt road where the stones
protrude as they did in his youth. He wonders if they're the same

ones he bobbed and weaved past in those barefoot days
as he played on his way to Jarrell's General Store.

The Petries lived over there where Carter Petrie raised
his fighting cocks. He would later lose an eye in a barroom

brawl. He now holds up inside the shack where he was
raised. Grandma Tucker's house was a half mile from there.

A squatter parks his trailer on her abandoned property where,
with her, the lad once gardened snap peas and corn, and

occasionally tomatoes when they made it through the blight
that seemed to come year to year. Just beyond was the old

swing bridge where he hung tight to the cables as he dangled
his feet over the deepest part of the river after rain. He was

five then. That wasn't far from where the older boys taught
him to catch crawdads in the fjord without getting pinched.

And just over the bridge those same boys taught him to bat
right-handed though he was as left-handed as they come.

As risky as the bridge is now, he crosses the rotting boards
toward Aunt Betty's house where he spent most of his

childhood days. How was it that after nearly thirty years he
had decided to see her one last time as she lay dying? There

is this—in the silence of time and the many moons that had passed, in his regrets, he would tell her how much he loved her

and how much she meant to him as a boy. She would clutch his hand, knowing at least for that moment, he meant it.

A Can of Chef Boyardee

All hinged on the mailbox in Carl Jarrell's General Store.
An envelope filled with ones and fives, or a money order
made out to Inez Tucker, Mom Tucker's other name.

We lived the myth of impoverished folks: a few bucks
gave us status, raise a finger to a can of Chef Boyardee
(the one with meatballs), and say, "I want that, and that ..."
until the cash ran out.

Mom Tucker washed clothes for the miners' wives; May
Dilly made curtains for them. None for us. The shanty
where we lived was windowless.

Like everything about us back then, we lived in an
un-curtained world.

I searched corners of the store where I had seen
the canvas bag before: *U.S. Post Office* inscribed.

Carl shook his head. Not today felt like forevermore.

Just like yesterday.

There was a secret knowledge to being poor back then.
A boy could disappear inside, become as nameless
as he wished, even when some kids thought they
saw him there.

A kid without rage or sorrow.
No regrets or wishing for anything beyond what he had:
that can of Chef Boyardee.

About Her Daily Chores

I swung her porch swing
with my feet. My grandmother sat
next to me. "Not too fast," she
admonished. "That's too much."

The swing to me was a thing of joy,
as though I could swing to the rafters
above. For her, a swing was not
for joy, but to complete her daily chores,
whether sitting on the porch
snapping snap peas, or cleaning
carrots from the garden for a stew.

I loved living with her for a time.
If only there'd been more of it.
When Aunt Mary Ann told her it was time
to give up keeping house and come live
with her in Baltimore, she acquiesced.

She never talked about West Virginia
again, or raising seven children,
and even sometimes their children.
She only talked about her daily chores.

When the Rose Died

The woman called mother spits to her side,
eyeing the floor where a small pool grows,
like scattered redbuds falling like petals
of innocence.

At seventeen, the drowsy days of play in a coal town
where she had lived and slipped through blades
of morning dew, all forgotten now.

While as the sun still ascends, it is not the sun she once sensed.
The rain that once renewed the mountains all around her
falls on streets of concrete here.

No more a sign of life that she once knew.

It will end soon, she says, this dispirited flesh that
cuts through those memories by fists that flick with venom
from my father called man. She told her story, always
in the present, time and again.

I sensed the sadness, anger that replaced those days
of innocence.

She has passed and I have aged beyond the wilting
of a rose. Once she was so beautiful, soon left unadorned.

In her memory, I slip through blades of morning dew
and seek the mountains every chance I can. It is there
I see her in her innocence, just over there.

Just over there.

Bleach, Just a Tad

"You kill the S.O.B, Nancy, and we'll watch the kids
while you're in jail," my mother's sisters said.

In later life she laughed, "I poured bleach
down his throat ... but just a tad."

"He was crazy, you know," she went on,
"but charming now and then."

How artfully they came to love and hate
with uniform intensity. Before he died,

long-since divorced, I looked in on him. Cancer
of the brain made him almost inaudible.

"Your mother was crazy, you know," he said
in a whispery tone. I nodded as I had with her.

The years had not changed either in regards
to their love or hate. Married, twice divorced,

I wondered what it took for them to make
it work as long as they had. "You need to rest,"

I said, wiped sweat from his forehead. His face
was gray, long fingers white as edelweiss. When

he died, a Bible and cross lay across his chest. He,
a transient, who knew in later life the angels awaited him.

My mother repeatedly expressed she was set to meet
her sisters in Paradise, if God willed it so. I was one

who believed if God existed, my reality was worlds apart
from Mom's and Dad's. But occasionally I revisit who we

were back then. I leave it to the life of our past ghosts.
Who were the bad guys, who were the innocent?

*Mom and Dad divorced when I was twelve. She was almost
comatose after that at times. I did most anything to get her
attention, which often worked against me.*

Fan Blades

Near her end of days, what was it that a mother
cared about her oldest son? Those many years that
had estranged them from the cord?

When I was young, sometimes all I knew of her was this—
she liked white dresses adorned with large flower
designs. We lived mainly in one room with a fan,
its two cracked blades turning around until it
almost cooled us down.

She stared at it like God himself was there
to give her guidance in her life.

It was I who cracked those blades, tossing anything
I could to seek her awareness now and then.

"My God, child! Don't you think I have enough on my
mind without this?" But then I fathomed only that I
needed her as she sat on her kitchen chair, hands
clasped at times to her face.

And yet, the damn fan blades kept turning around.

As we aged those fan blades were barely a memory
for a while. She read *People* magazine to find out
how rich folks lived, and I went off to war to protect
us from our enemies.

Yes, in her final days, I wondered what my mother
thought of who I had become. But in her room in aided
care, she stared at the blades as the fan spun around.

Silently.

At peace with what it was.

LIFE
in
DRY CREEK,
WEST VIRGINIA
(Friendly View Village)

Before The Whitesville
Mine Explosion, 2010

Where We Lived
(Friendly View, Dry Creek, WV)

We called it home, Friendly View, a village near where
Dry Creek mountains grieved for ghosts of family miners
buried there. And the women folk yelled to God to rid

them of their rage for a coal company's indifference.
A few miles away, Mt. View Elementary School stood,
hill-bound, overlooking coal camps, rutted roads,

and rotten clapboard habitats where potbelly stoves
spun black coal smoke for heat, and wood burner stoves
cooked Chef Boyardee spaghetti and summer kale.

Ms. Jones, our first grade teacher, as much as
said to parents, *Soiled clothes are the Devil's work;
cleanliness, God's temple.* I wore clean ones,

hand-me-downs from Cousin Joe, a year ahead of me.
Frayed homemade quilts warmed us from the winter
freeze. Lightbulbs, dull-yellow; when some popped,

spurred our early exits to bed. We, at the bottom
of a hill in winter, felt the snow drifts' wrath. We cut
a footpath up a steep incline to make it to a bus

that whined but always made it to its destiny.
We had visions that those days would end.
We always wished for things we couldn't have.

*Second Place Recipient,
West Virginia Writers Contest, 2020*

A Place Where We All Belonged
(Friendly View, a Dry Creek,
West Virginia Village)

There were no violins in Friendly View, no ballets.
Only men dressed in dungarees paying reverence

to the songs their daddies played and feet-tapping
to the rhythms of the fiddles handed down.

The women joined in too, set aside their autoharps
and foot-shuffled across the warped porch slats

until the moon met the mountain peaks.
The old house still stands, silent in the shadows

of a sun going down. I don't know if I recall
it all just right, those lives where hope was sung

in songs and we all belonged, and laughter came
so easily, that family of country folks. I miss them so.

The young had a different outlook on Dry Creek
than their elders. Elders stayed to make the best of a bad
situation through their humor and music. In the fifties
and beyond, the young often left in their teens.

Dry Creek,
Just a Place to Be From

The smoky-fog of clouds awaited
the morning dew. The chill revealed
the character of those who stayed.

I knew I would eventually escape to concrete
lands, city streets, and avenues with trees
lined up like soldiers in drab green garb.

I was serene in that small village,
Maybe too much so—a child who
watched the miners die year-to-year.

Oh, so slowly. There were the Petries,
Tuckers, Jarrells, Aliffs, all gone,
decades ago. There's no one now

left to carry on. Their youth, still young,
moved on where they were quick to say,
"Dry Creek is just a place to be from."

Do You Really Want to Do This Again?

The women sweep the porch where the dust settles
back and the kids hardly ever bathe their miner-like
charred gray faces. You can smell their small breaths
a yard away.

The eyelids of widows burdened down in tears for a
century. It is the land of those unsleeping women
wondering what's next with four mouths to feed.

Dads are seeping out of death like roulette wheels
every time they go into the mines. But that's what
men do there, one blow away from the eternal.

For men fortunate enough to escape the rage
of the mines, black lung is next for them.
It calls when they are fifty-ish.

This is a place that questions the sanity
of men, the twisting hills and thoroughfares,
the pulse of morning fog that dampens
the brain, that eats away the dreams
of the poor.

Poverty by no other name endures.

It is the land of worn hands and no promises.
It is the land that would rather throw you away
than give in an inch.

It is a land when night falls and the blackness
as black as any place on Earth asks,
"Do you really want to do this again?"

In Memory of the White Church
Dry Creek, WV

Desolate the surroundings where I kneel
to a God I feel does not exist.

It reminds me of my childhood
in Dry Creek where miners' wives prayed,

only to hear their men had died
when mine buttresses gave in.

"Where were you then?" I ask,
knowing no answer will come.

"Swear to me you'll do better
in the future," I say, taking on a deity,

more phantom than holiness.
"Are you there?" I ask honestly.

I pause a moment, rise from a dirt patch
where the white church use to be.

Back to Dry Creek, WV

Timeless, it seems, the stream
I visited recently, where I used
to fish in my youth. I strode

about aimlessly, hoping to find life
somewhere among the abandoned
homes. Arthur Aliff's doghouses

still stand but they are empty now.
Chains, some remain, that once
tethered his pack of hounds.

Boards, so weathered, may be
decent firewood as they fall
from their fastenings.

A fifty-something Ford frame
rusts alongside the road.
Nothing's left but tattered

remembrances. I'll walk alone
through this abandonment
until evening comes when

the mountains and forest grow
so dark, they suspend humankind's
ability to tread, even wearily.

Those who owned these lands long ago,
return it now, where it belongs rightfully
to the Dry Creek overgrowth.

We Played in the Snowdrifts

We played in the snowdrifts when winter came.
Good sense was not among our attributes.

Hardiness was. We faced up to adversity
as though it were a paltry thing. When darkness

came, we played still among the hills where we
saw each other by the whiteness, bright by moonlight,

and heard each other only by our laughs. The unbroken
sounds of all this led to a clanship we would never know

again, when we left for city work where the folks seemed
high and mighty. I cannot say how downcast I became

in this other life when the veil of success perplexed me so.
Oh, yes, I did succeed among the greed and back-biting

troupes of youth where self-importance reigned. I can barely
recall the friendships of my youth. But when the snow storms

come, I walk among them, laugh at this continuing intrigue
of how a city society measures the making of a man.

Hopefulness

A boy sits by the side of the road and waits. This is where
his mother will turn onto the old dirt road to come for him.

She *hopes to see him soon*, she says in letters he gathers
from the General Store. There, the post office is another

hopeful place where months have turned to years.
"It's only a matter of time," his Grandma Tucker says

as she gives him change for an RC Cola and Pet vanilla
ice cream. He holds the money tightly in his hand. What

does *matter of time* mean? It puzzles him. He sits a while
longer, throwing stones across the road before he goes,

before his grandmother wonders where he is. The store
is nearly a mile away. What happens if his mother comes

before he returns? For the moment, it is a reason
to wait, as though the world is on his side.

Leaving Some Things Unsaid

What memory of a boy at five does a man at seventy-five recall?
Maybe the red wagon where the boy sits, waits by the roadside.

His mother will surely come today. Like a mamma-bird who
has left the nest to gather her fare for the little one.

Hide him in these hills, protect him like a nest embedded
deep inside the evergreens.

Maybe it's just the memory of Dry Creek. West Virginia,
a land as beautiful, bountiful in its beauty—the mountains

blue in the morning mist—as it is a consumer of men
laid down in the mines. Coal River flows there, a slow

crawl where the current sways among the curvatures,
where the crawdads peek from beneath the rocks as

though they have no place else to go. And in between
the dales are the meadows where settlers set up shanties

a hundred years ago. I loved those fields back then.
The chatters of the other children; some felt as abandoned

as I did. It is a scene, in and out of reality now. Death
and life cross paths here and there. Decay, as compelling

as it is, leaves a man with gentler memories, mostly,
of what was. The honey bees that fill the fields and how

they live in such serenity where it is easy to believe
how every creature on that clover lives forever,

and a mother is somewhere just beyond the bend.
Where did the mother go? Protect the boy from what?

Sometimes it's best to believe the world is beautiful.
Sometimes it's best to leave some things unsaid.

Decaying Pine Planks
(Fifty-Five Years after the
Farmington, WV Mine Exploded)

A boy tiptoes over decaying pine planks
past the rusted chains where the porch swing
seated migrants' heirs for years.

Where folks appeared with picks and shovels
a hundred forty years ago.

Now gone.

It is the likes of those who mined the mines
will never see again. What is a village without inhabitants?

No poverty lives on without dweller residents.
No fair wages sought in distress.
No woe to keep the women folk awake at night
when the coal company owned everything they had.

So curious, how self-enslaved the tenants had become.

None left for better lives, but endured
the village as their home to raise their children
just like them in hopes for generations to come.

What does an old man recall of a childhood long ago?
The past is never just the past, only to be relived again.

The future has no meaning here and illusions never cease
for those who fall for the sleight of hand.
Coal companies move on.
Dead miners, only numbers on the news.

The Abandoned Village

It's hard to say when the grief began and older children
left the land. Scattered homes, dilapidated now, grass

grown foot-high among the weeds, it is more a place
where crows caw and winds whisper in solitude. Where

once gardens grew, the soil gave way to kindred weeds,
a few wild flowers here and there. No disparity between

overgrown old gardens and gravesites. There was never
grandeur here. Religious folk, they only wished what came

next beyond their burial place. They came with thoughts
of independent power only to leave the Earth in disarray,

disorderly mortality, a coal miner's resting place. Scots-Irish
blood, disdain to be mastered, yet mastered everyone.

What was it they willed to conquer if not the land? But
the land is a patient foe that will prevail among the plunder

where men will mingle with brief ill-gotten gains. What
tyranny is this: the land and all wild life it preserved, or man

who impaired what wasn't his? The crows and winds knew.

Endless Drift

Curious, a boy age five stared at a streambed,
    a flow of the river, with such intent.
  It was his river of forgetting,

in its endless drift. When he grew to be
an old man, he recalled how the river

held sway over who he was,
    forgetting all else, recalling
  only that it was beautiful.

Everyday Encounters with the Past

When I was young, I never read books
about boys being abused. Even now, I
leave Dickens to Dickens.

I wrote often about the abandoned and
mistreated until my fingers grew
stiff as drumsticks, pounding away.

Those were the '80s.

I surmised then the tales were only
meaningful to me. The abuse as a child,
my mother finally going insane when

she too was battered by my dad.
How narrow the scope, I thought,
how small the mind that mainly
continued on this motif.

I read more of those authors who
moved on to greater themes.

It was all there in Steinbeck all the time.
The poverty. The geographic cures.
The Land.

It reminded me of my hitchhiking days,
mainly in the '70s, revisiting some communities,
and the village haven I once knew.

It was a slow dance how life was abandoned
there in time, save those folks who chose to ride
it out until nothing remained. The days
of Scot-Irish bobs and weaves through life
that disappeared.

The mountains themselves now displayed
where a patch of land once swelled with gardening,
and the late leaves of old oak trees refused to give in.

And the swallows made their beds in abandoned
habitats. The moss cast over the ruins,
and the rusted gates crumpled everywhere
that could no longer keep anything in or out.

While the snap-crack of lightening severed
thick tree trunks from violent winds; the fragile
fields survived.

Rapids uncoiled over rocks and boulders,
the river amassed since ancient times.

And I wondered if there would be new inhabitants
in years to come? Or would the village headstones
be the only epithet for our old village there?

At times I thought I'd return, this land as beautiful as
destitute. This place, like a Steinbeck journey's end,
that once protected me.

We are bruised, this land and I, but we are
on the mend.

Time is not the only salve.
Nor an aging memory.
And the slow flow of the river
can only do so much to clean up
what man has done.

It has been a journey between love and hate.
Travel between kindness and rage.

The sound of a baby's first scream.
The way a mother weeps for what is,
protects against those in and out
of darkness days.

It is a quick go-round, this presence.
The everyday encounters with the past,
sometimes that come back instantly,
sometimes years and then again,
sometimes a kaleidoscope,
broken pieces, some that will never mend.

And the fear of what may come calling next.

Returning to a Place Called Youth

Spring tends to its new blossoming. The mists
of March showers can be seen everywhere.

If there is a reason to spend time among the
mountains, it's in this time of serenity.

It is a jealous wilderness that prefers the solitude,
spends its time nurturing the mountain blooms,

breathes out the songs of the pine-winds where
the breeze chooses new melodies. My stay here

was like a mountain nest when I was young.
The delight of those times cannot be reborn.

It is like the hawk that comes back to roost that
finds its nest unkempt and mother gone.

So now I linger here for a spell where our gardens
and fields have long been buried beneath the oatgrass

and a thousand wildflowers. Soon, an old man stands,
rushes to say, "Wait, old chap. I've been here long

enough. I'll go with you!" in time to find it is only me,
this moment, this hour, that will never return again.

If
THAT
DOESN'T
GIVE YOU
a
CHILL

If That Doesn't Give You a Chill

It's over a hundred degrees in an Okinawan Quonset hut,
no air to speak of. The warehouse guys and I are coming
back to where we live for lunch.

It's 1966.

There is a new guy on a bunk. His name is Murph. He only
stares at the ceiling, doesn't give us eye contact when we walk
in. His face sinews twitch slightly. Otherwise, he's still.

In several weeks he will confide in me. I don't know why,
but only me. He was a machine gunner in 'Nam. He killed
what he thought were four Viet Cong only to find when
the battle ended, that they were four children.

The Marine Corps will give him rest, fill him full
of Thorazine and try to send him back. Machine gunners
are a premium. They don't know just then ... he's done.

I am eighteen then. I send machine guns and machine
gun rounds to Vietnam. It dawns on me; I am also one
to blame for killing those children.

All my life, well-meaning folks will say, "Aren't you glad
you weren't in Vietnam?"

I'm there some nights. Nightmares take on the same
terrain. Sleep doesn't come easily.

Now at seventy-five, at night I still stay awake at times.
I see four faces, blood on all of them. Their clothes
blotched in blood as well.

If that doesn't give you a chill, what will?

What will?

A Few Shots of Gin

Haas says we need to stop at the club
and have a few shots of gin. I'm hesitant.

"The brass can't smell it," he says.
We're checking out, going stateside.

I just turned nineteen, Haas twenty-one.
He tells me his job last year in 'Nam emerged,

recovering body parts borne out by men's
identities, to lay them out in body bags.

Even then he grins. He always seems to grin.
So I concede. He is the experienced one.

I will learn sometime in life when to follow
and when to lead. But today I am sitting

in a bar in Okinawa drinking more shots
of gin than I think I should, following

Haas's encouragement. Our company
officer will say, "You two are shit-faced!"

He tells Haas he will go home by plane.
"You," he says, "for your stupidity, sixteen

days on the *General John B. Pope*, to think
of what you did." On that ship, I learn

to comprehend the detriment of following,
when one thinks he should know otherwise.

But I question if a man's life isn't really
a roll of the dice, one shamed by drinking

a few shots of gin, and how one lives
with his stint as a steward of body bags.

GEOGRAPHICAL CURES

from the

PAIN

of the

PAST

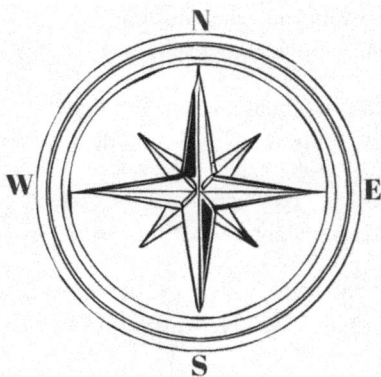

These are poems about hitchhiking, bus rides, and a poem about another former Marine (drifter) attempting a geographical cure, a term used often to describe traveling anywhere to attempt to alleviate painful memories and past events, or at times a way the penniless get around.

Hitchhiking through Tulsa

In Tulsa, an old Ford pickup truck squeals up ahead,
right signal blinking. I rush up to the truck.

"Where you going?" The driver asks.
"Vietnam," I say, tongue in cheek.

I see a shotgun mounted on his rear window.
"Get in," he says. "I'll take you part way."

He plays my game. "We're going to win this war
with guys like you." He goes on. "Got time for a drink?"

"Sure," I say. At this point I have time
before checking into Camp Pendleton.

Two months of guerilla warfare drills
in front of me in California clime this time
of year. It'll be ninety-something degrees.

"Several miles away we pull into the parking
lot of a private club, *Members Only,* the sign

on the door cautions. "He's with me," the driver says.
Several drinks and midnight nears. "I'd best be on my way,"

I say, seabag in hand. "Seriously," the bartender asks,
"you're not twenty-one …?" He winks. I smile and leave

without saying I'm eighteen. Drinking age: twenty-one.
I never knew the name of one person in that bar.

But that night I found out what a patriot was. Now
at seventy-five, I still revere the men in that bar.

Hitchhiking Past the Painted Desert

In awe of reds, purples, golds, and blues,
my senses succumb to this desert view.

A Navajo lady picks me up in Tulsa and leaves
me here. Everywhere we stop, with her camera,

roll of film in hand—she asks strangers to take
a photo of us. Hand on my shoulder, she smiles.

She wants to remember me, a young Marine.
I am thankful she allows me to be a part of what

she values, one of many patriots I meet along
the way. I am in uniform. More importantly,

I see what she sees most evenings. She gives me
the gift of memory. More precious than *owning* things,

that land is only rented for an instance—the sun,
the stars, the moon, constellations of the heavens

will retain claim over time and the elements.
"Watch out for the sidewinders," she says and drives

down an arid road. This is the reservation where she lives.
My will to stay here is strong, to watch the colors

of the desert change as the sun falls beyond the hills.
But I will move on eventually, another ride, another town.

I revisited that desert in my sixties, paid a private driver
to take me on a hill there at sunset. "Is this what you saw?"

he asked. Speechless, I nodded, teary-eyed. I imagined
that my Navajo lady was still alive and that I would thank her.

That, beyond war, I would find peace and serenity
in lands like this beyond the valueless nature of conflict.

Hitchhiking through
Beaver Falls, Pennsylvania

It's 1972. I'm on my way to Purdue to check in, a new
student on the G.I. Bill and graduate stipend.

I thumb through Beaver Falls. Before long, a guy
in a soiled T-shirt stops, eight track tape blaring beside him.

"Where you going?" he asks, like a coroner, emotionless.
I hesitate to get in, but it's two a.m. Chances of getting a ride

this late, waning. "Indiana," I say. "How 'bout you?"
"Anywhere," he says. "I just ride at night." The smell

of mustiness reviles me momentarily. Then I hardly notice it.
"I care for my mom throughout the day," he says. As I listen,

I realize this is his shackle-less time, this shift worker, unpaid,
no reprieve for anything but the sound of an engine spitting out

tailpipe oil, and him, hanging on to a boom box that bellows
a Frank Sinatra tune, *I Did It My Way*, as though Frank were

really there. He drives me far beyond Beaver Falls. I motion
to him. "I'll get out here." He pulls over, only stares forward

at the road ahead. I swear he may have driven me
to West Lafayette. As I watch the tailpipe smoke

spewing, I imagine him lost in a night, like all nights,
consumed by a song he'll never carry out.

Hitchhiking through Columbus

"If I catch you here again," the cop says, "I'll take you in."
My second go-round with him. Hitchin' on the interstate

tends to be intense at times. I say, "Okay," but when he's gone,
I'll move on down the main highway once again.

"You can use the exit ramp," the cop says, frowning at me.
But that's like, no ride at all. But I play the game with a half

dozen other guys. "Want a toke, man?" One pothead lies
in gravel with his limp thumb pointing out at cars to come.

I shake off the offer, check out the road conditions
down the interstate. No cops in sight, but they like to hide

between truckers and me with no CB, nothing to link up
with them; I take another go at it. I rush to a site where

no other hikers will risk a ride in a Columbus cop's van.
If caught a third time, I sense I'll get just a ride.

The cop pulls beside me, cuffs in hand. "What'd I tell you?"
He shakes his head, as if to say he's seen the likes of me

many times before. If I didn't believe in Jesus, I might have
just then. A young woman in a VW van pulls over and screams,

"He's with me." Maybe she didn't have the looks of a movie
star but just then she was my Marilyn Monroe. The cop

releases me and says, "I better never see you here again."
I nod respectfully and engage my new friend. "Where you off to?"

I ask. "Fredericksburg, Virginia," she says. "Richmond here,"
I say. I toss my old Marine Corps seabag in the back and listen

to the radio, "Me and Bobby McGee" blasting until the
speakers shake. I go to speak, but she's so stoked she isn't listening

to anything but Joplin. But if she really wants, I think,
I'll be her Bobby McGee.

Hitchhiking to Purdue

New to the Midwest, hands raw with innocence,
unaware what icy air could do, I yearn to feel
the touch of fingers on my cheeks, other than

a burn like frozen fire. Frost-flowery ground
shrouds itself in ice. The haze of occasional
snow makes distant roads feel more distant

than nearby. Nightclubs closed for the night,
thumbing at two a.m. from Indianapolis to Purdue,
I only wish someday to smell the scent
of a rose and feel my fingers again.

Hitchhiking through Charleston, WV
(1973)

I hitchhike through Charleston, long-haired mane,
shoulder length. Tar-heat from the road, my nostrils

heave in this dust-laden air. Wheels of nineteen fifty- and
sixty-something Chevys, Fords, all American made,

spin on roads beside a stop sign where I stand,
beyond the general stores, beyond ageless coal mines,

beyond ancient knolls, beyond the vales.
I write on a soiled cloth bag I carry—"I am one of you."

Old sedans dash past me, some laughing, some scowling,
at the thought of such absurdity. I am just a character,

a bad scene, this Sunday evening for folks coming home
from church. Foreigners, or long-haired American ones,

aren't welcome here. I could have stayed on the interstate,
but chose to see an America I thought I once knew, where

I had hoped to be embraced as one of them. Maybe it was
wrong to ask so much of those in these insulated hills. I bear

my own brand of faith, that however diverse, we are
a community of one. But this day will test my faith, as I wait

well into night before a kindly stranger asks me where I'm going.
It is a good night for riding over winding roads, where

as a child I grew up where bobcats roamed and Coal River
provided swimming holes. Maybe I came to reclaim

my heritage, but the theater of life, absurd, ironic, presents
me with a different script, torn between who I am and was.

There are no words to reconcile who one wants to be, and
heading down a different road toward one's next destiny.

Passing through America
(Or, Praying from a Greyhound Bus)

Passing abandoned hotels, likely by-the-hour
bordellos, past the factories with their blackened
skies, past the homeless in their box bins, winding

miles past the place I came from. I wonder what
life will become. No one's blaming anyone.
My father, dead, smoked Chesterfields, non-filters,

knowing of carcinogens. My mother forgets who
she is, forgets the man she ran from time and again.
The bus was our main means back then.

They say time heals all wounds. Let them have their say.
I just stare out the window and think, *this too shall pass*,
these memories, before we reach somewhere I've never been.

Praying for a bit of joy in life, I laugh and think a Greyhound bus
is no place for epiphanies. Knowing me, some would decree
that could be the miracle of miracles.

The Theater Called Bus

A tattoo of a fish swims up a young girl's thigh.
A guy with dreads waves his head like Stevie Wonder
without music or instrument.

An old man grazes his lower lip, smells of pee-covered
jeans, T-shirt coffee stained. And a man, fiftyish, from time
to time downs the hair of the dog.

I watch us disappear in shadows of bridge trestles
that appear as skeletons. Half-eaten honey buns
degenerate from a woman who disembarked last night.

Acquaintances quarantined in collective idleness
seem oblivious to the dead fish smell, like an old
mattress, in aisles stained from past scenes.

It is near noon. With no place to go, I wait
for the blur of pine trees and concrete passing
by to take me somewhere offstage.

Neither comedy nor tragedy, the play will resume.
We stop momentarily, wait for the players backstage
to get on, undiscovered talent waiting to perform the real,
                                        the imaginary.

Drifter

My Audi Fox hums on I-84, coming home
from U. of Oregon, windshield wipers slapping
ice to-and-fro.

Strange theater to think
just three months ago someone stole
my manuscripts, me a writer without a name
embossed on printed pages.

I'll be home in days,
wherever that is.

I have no address. Just an MFA dropout
who had hoped to meet Ken Kesey,
One Flew over the Cuckoo's Nest fame.

Even the trees are frozen over.
Yet I spin wheels, listen to Oldies that leave
me wondering who I am, fifteen years
since my Marine Corps time in the Orient,
sending machine guns, ammo rounds,
to killing fields in 'Nam.

Still trying to get over those days.

Audi, don't go into a tailspin,
not now. I hear the echo of tires
in mountains nearby.

No cars, no trucks, come west. Who would
have guessed an interstate could freeze?

Yet, I drive faster, maybe recklessly to get on with it.
One hand on the wheel, the other wiping
fog from a car that fails to defrost,
drive cockeyed—spots of black ice glow
like water on the road.

No telling when a slide will take me into a ravine.
Up ahead, a man maybe my age, in tattered
overcoat shuffles feet, his shoulders nearly
parallel to the ground.

I slide beyond him,
shut down Neil Young's "It's Only Castles Burning,"
tap on my windshield. "Hey, where to?"

He doesn't look up at me but stops. "Omaha."
"Okay," I say.

Without another word, he lobs his pack, old
field coat, soil-smattered, on my backseat,
slouches down on the passenger side.

"I don't do no sex thing," he says.

"Nor do I," I say, slowly grinding
on gravel back on Highway 84.

A thousand miles pass without a word.
I stop for gas, buy him some nachos
with cheese. He eats two, maybe three,
drops the rest between his knees on my
floorboard. I want to play Joplin,
"Bobby McGee," but think it best not to,
but keep my eyes on the highway, reading
mileage signs: Omaha 208.

My mind, wary, no shuteye, I ask him,
"Do you drive?"

"Sho," he says curtly. I give him
the keys without looking down at him,
close my eyes. From the passenger side,
I feel a rumble beneath my feet, look up
to find my Audi among old cornstalks.

"I thought you could drive!" I snap at him.
"Not like this!" Maybe it's the ice.

I don't know what that means but take the keys,
drive on. Omaha can't be soon enough.

When the ramp arrow points,
Omaha, I simply say, "This is it."

"I know," he says, grabs his pack.
Not a *Thank you*. Not another word.

I look back. He disappears across a road
where I assume a younger man once lived.

I never see his eyes nor know his name,
but remember him for day-old nachos
and cheese permeating my floorboard.
Remember him my next stop, his tattered
overcoat in my back seat.

I check pockets for some sense of who
he may be. Only an insignia, Globe and Eagle.
Former Marine. Strange theater, it seems.

A Morning Walk

There is nothing I love more than this—
a morning walk through the blue mist
of the mountains where the clouds meet
the peaks, and earthly songs begin the day.

In the distance, the rooster joins in at early light,
and the random baritones of the bullfrogs play along.
The crickets chirp in the after-rain. The morning glories

come to life from their nightly rest. And in the open
fields, the scent of sun-drenched lavender still lingers
near my path.

A lush heaviness of fertile pines seems to be everywhere,
as fall nears its close.

Then there are the lone maples that preen their leaves,
leaving limbs half-clad. Even as they lie nearly bare,

I have seen much less beauty in my life,
their yellow-red blush, so innocent. If you go there,

stop by the rim of wetlands where the beavers busily
build their domes, and the egrets find fingerlings

for sustenance. And you will see an old carving
on the largest oak: *I was once here.*

No matter. You have seen what you need to see.
No need to know who I am.

Portal of Stars

The first time I saw neon was when I was seven
from the backseat of Dad's '49 Ford.

He had collected us like chattel, my mother
and me, from the West Virginia mountains where
the peaks were dressed in gray clouds half the time,
hiding the shades of green-bluish pines.

Dad wanted us to be family-like.
We never were.

I was the son of the mountains where my
grandmother raised me most of my first seven
years among the breadth, the portal of stars.

In my late teens and twenties, I hitchhiked
for spells to get outside myself, to get away
from the mindlessness of Dad's earlier rage.
His abuse.

It rarely worked.

Now in my seventies, I live outside a forest
where green-bluish pines recall who I am
(no neon signs for miles), and the portal
of stars beckons me.

I still miss the mountains though that spoke
to me in wordless serenity and fathered me
in silent whispers to calm down when all
around me all was chaos back then.

But I am family now with the green-bluish
pines by day and portal of stars at night.
They protected me from all that neon meant
to me back then.

And that they still do.

THOSE
WHO TRIED
TO HELP
(Bless Them All)

The Eviction

I was kindling for my mother's wrath—not so much
at me, but at the universe.

"Your father's not coming back," she said,
"and the landowner wants us out."

It was 1960 then. As my aunt picked us up
to take us to her row house in Baltimore,

my mother left a stack of bills on a small table
near the door that I presume, looking back,

would be sent, *No Forwarding Address*. And
I would learn the lessons that every twelve

year old poor boy grasps: the space you
embrace will never uncover who you are if you

move fast enough. The wheels of my aunt's 1950
Chevy moved on, and it would move on again

in time, indefinitely through the sphere of our
broken dreams until we had no dreams at all.

Lie Still, Young West Virginian

Lie still, young West Virginian. You, lifeless
in an alleyway behind a D.C. bar, far from the land
of bobcats, rainbow trout, and blue-green mountains,
partly hidden by the fog and morning dew.

Lie still, young West Virginian. The city isn't done
with you yet, you in your tattered blazer, the only
coat you own, pebbles in your pockets.
How did they get there? you may ask.

Lie still, young West Virginian, on this steel gurney
which holds your gangly frame. You look so feeble,
pale. A doctor will finally say, "A couple found
you, blue, almost without pulse. You're free to go."

Walk gingerly, young West Virginian, past cracked walls
of commerce, Lafayette Park where the homeless reside,
Four Georges restaurant where presidents dine, Mass
Avenue where diplomats unravel foreign policy.

Walk gingerly, young West Virginian. This is not the land
of rainbow trout and mountain streams but of brick barriers,
urban sprawl, where the rhythm quickens. You
don't understand. One you will never understand.

> *This is a poem about my early twenties and living in the*
> *suburbs/cities when those geographical cures hadn't worked*
> *and I hadn't adjusted to suburban/city life (nor have I now).*
> *I started going through a series of psychiatrists, social worker*
> *therapists, etc. during and after this period.*

Bruises

Lie still, old man. Those bruises are as faint as they'll ever be.
You survived (but time is not a clock that rewinds).

All who have passed and once scarred you, you gave them peace.
Living forgiveness is a generous thing.

Lie still, old man. Your pain will remain for the bigness and the smallness
for what you've done. (You are not the only one with welts to fade.)

The injuries you aroused among your peers may be a birth
that has a lasting tale. It is never a story of one.

Every story has a theme. We are never really the players we think we are.
The rhythm sometimes beats of love ... and insanity.

Lie still, old man. The hardship has been a way to presence
and peace. Listen to those who've learned to love you.

They know best who you are.

A Place Where Kindness Is

Dreams work to mend the mind in disrepair.
It is where the sleeping garden grows.

Only for the longing, it is where best to come
to know the nature of a rose, where imagination

learns to pluck its weeds. It is a place of ponds
where the whitest lilies dwell. You can swim

there in serenity. I did at times. Nowhere
nearby will you find a hopeless future there.

Listen to the waterfalls cascade. They will never dry within you.

Listen

It is a place where kindness is.

Don't waste time otherwise. It is your world
to dream as you will, even as the morning
sun shines deep within, even as you waken
to who you want to be.

Even at times when you have trouble listening.

> *After ten years of therapy, I began to understand that the most*
> *powerful aspect of life was finding kindness where I could. In the*
> *volunteer work I engaged in, young folks often asked me why I did*
> *what I did for them. My answer typically was,*
> *"I'm not doing this for you; I'm doing this for me."*

What Then?

Lost wisdom, the slowing opaque spaces
in my mind; bleak reminders in a universe
where more darkness exists than sparks
of stars.

I reminisce where I can—a learned man
whose walls buttress of old degrees.

What value do they leave behind to a mind
that's left to fend for recalling anything,
that these days would come, so cruel
to creep, tick by tick, so silently?

Still there is this, the love of kin and friends,
less time to think of who I used to be.

If it were not so, what then?

The Weapon of a Memory

The weapon of a memory resides with my gloom,
the quiet pain that never leaves, the whisper of rage
of echoes long ago—violence has so many names,
as does the salve that heals. I still wish for the boy
who visits here. I wish for him melodic choirs and
delicate strings. But time disobeys the man who longs
to unwind tempos of the past. Days promise no easy
tomorrows. There were fists that showed no mercy back
then against a young boy's ears. Only a reel for future
memories, the mind's words or a poet's tongue keeping
time with a dark heartbeat. "Do not linger here," a kinder
voice repeats. "Seventy years lived like this is long enough."

A Neighbor's Gift

My father, age fourteen, worked
on the boxcars in the railyards
in Richmond, VA. Calloused hands
for a boy turned young man.

His father, dying, diseased
from veins somewhat collapsed, lost
muscle mass, lay in bed for seven years
where his sweat smelled of stale garlic.

When Depression came, the family kept
the bank at bay. The farmhouse shed
its paint and gutters held last year's leaves.
My father and siblings wore old clothes

year after year. The garden supported them.
Tomatoes, beans, squash, and greens.
At fifty-five, my father, one who rarely cried,
cried one day pertaining to a lady

who lived down the street from him.
When he was four, she had given him
a red wagon. Thinking back, I was a distant
son who never gave him more than that.

The Neighbor in Need Club

Al, a used car salesman, created the Neighbor in Need
Club to help those dependent on alcohol or drugs.

There were those who guffawed over his style
of salesmanship. Long-winded, rambled on.

He beckoned me one day to help him on a call.
Dubious, I said yes nonetheless with no idea
of his plan to help a man in need.

When we arrived, a woman, maybe fifty-five, said,
"You want to help the son of a bitch, go right ahead!
I've had it with him!"

The stench from outside overpowering, we walked
into a bedroom where a man lay in his feces, some
caked on.

"Undress, except your skivvies," Al instructed me.
"We'll get him in the shower now."

This man who others found amusing, I now saw
as a man possessed to help someone else,
without the least bit of interest in himself.

"We're here to get you to the hospital," Al told
the man. "I don't want to go," the man said.

"What you want and what you need are two
different things," Al replied, as we half-dragged
him to the shower.

My clothes, half-soaked from my skivvies when
I put them back on, it didn't matter.

Several days afterward, he came into the club dressed
in a clean sport shirt and slacks, his hair slicked back. He
looked like a man who wanted self-respect again.

And Al? He never seemed to wonder what folks thought
of him, or if they laughed at his style. He went on helping
folks gain their self-respect. And what I wanted more than

anything after that was what Al had.

The Communion

Communion of a man and a boy of their past,
spheres of sadness—both concur. There is
a certain whimsy in all of this, what one felt,
what one can only imagine was real or supposed.
Was it the boy, later a man who longed for a father
who would throw him a ball? The layers of regret
that passed again and again, from childhood
to man, arising from all of that, seeking out
something so simple, yet so complex—just
watching young folks on the field, parents living
through their children's dreams. "That's right, son ...
nice catch! There is magic in those hands!" a father
screams. A boy would run beyond the boundaries
of that field to catch that ball. A boy envies what
he can't have, and a man can only replace the reality
of his past so much before it is no longer his.
But there is never an age when a man won't
revisit his former dreams, and play the same
game repeatedly, hoping this time the sadness
will subside, beyond the realm of that playing field.

Last Gardens of My Imagining

In midlife, I couldn't have wanted another
life other than the one I dreamed—a full
belly, writing poetry, wearing clothes

that fit the times. But life has a way of eluding
everything we want, spending those midlife years
harvesting a modest annuity for my final days

and counseling executives who listened less
to me but only testaments to their policies. Now
past seventy, I write bad verse, eat too much, and

gather old clothes to give away I wore nearly half
a century ago, when I had that youthful dream. I
delight in a wife who supports what must appear

as insanity, my days spent closed-door in a room,
listening to the beat of past rock bands, and writing
verses that cripple my hand. It is my fate, the simple-

minded guy I've become with a few regrets, finding
truth by tilling words that grow among last gardens
of my imagining, tending to this last fruitful time.

Divorce

I light a cigarette
     and watch the smoke
        turn playfully into a quiet tune.
I want to sing it,
     but it is gone
         lost in the silence
of an empty room.

"Divorce" and "Watching the Waves Come In"

first appeared in Wild Goose Poetry Review, *No. 33, Fall 2017*

"Divorce", describes a scene at the end of my first marriage when I told my wife that she could take any of the furniture she wanted. When I came home later, all she had left me was a living room chair, a small kitchen table with two chairs, and a single bed upstairs. I wrote "Divorce" in less than a half hour afterwards.

Watching the Waves Come In

There are rarely wedding cakes
for second marriages.
There's more the "Let's get on with this,
and hope we'll make good what we couldn't
with the other spouse."

"We're no virgins to this," I said
to my wife-to-be days before we wed.
She nodded, agreed this was an
experiment, her parents relieved
she was going to marry someone
with a full set of teeth.

"Besides," she said, "they think
you're clever."
I said she had a nice body
and hoped she remained trim,
at least until our fifties, me

thirty-six, she thirty-four.
"Fair enough," she said. "But
you're sporting a small paunch.
I would expect you to get rid of it."
When it came time, the Justice
of the Peace read: "Do you take this man …"

"Of course I do," she said.
"Let's get on with it."
"Do you take this woman ..."
"Ditto what she said," I said.
After the vows and a cup of joe
in a coffee shop, we've come to know
the other, inside out, for more than thirty years.

Not so long ago while on a tour,
at dinner with a couple older than us,
I sat feeling the ocean breeze,
watching wave after wave come to shore.

"He used to be handsome," my wife said to them.
I grinned and learned long ago when to soldier on,
when to just watch the waves come in.

*"Watching the Waves Come In" is Kate describing
our wedding to an older couple while on vacation in Costa Rica.
Married in 1985. This was twenty years later.*

Where Home Is

She waits for the nurse to give her meds.
She has no will, no memory, to take them

on her own. She opens wide at her caretaker's
gentle command. She smiles at the "nice man,"

she calls him. Just when it seems she is
worsening, a speech therapist asks her

questions to which she replies, "I learned
that in the third or fourth grade." As if to say

I will humor you, she answers anyway.
She will walk down the hallway time and again.

No more days of asking, "When can I go home?"
She is settled now. She is one of a klatch

of women her age who dine together each evening.
Who beyond the memory-less days, who beyond

life in their past, know mostly there is now, and
monikers on their doors that show who they are
and where home is.

Just Be a Friend
(My Tribute to Barbara Henn)

True friend who asked so modestly of me:
"Just be a friend."

We search in life for what we treasure,
filling needs from emptiness to joy.

Mind and heart in sync with what we
we hunger for.

There is peace in all of this.

The friendship that rarely asks why.
What is reaped in all of this in absence
and in mystery of why the friendship
succeeds, yes thrives.

It is the sweetness of the charity.
It is what she's sown.

A friend steeped in helping me
un-depress, borne into the age
of the elderly, where gray-to-white
ignites the hair progressing day-to-day:

(Call it ripeness.)

She spurs this old emerging poet
to stay attentive to his dreams,
prods him at times to be more than
he thinks he is.

And all the time, he feels so strongly
that she is just so much more of a friend
than he ever deemed imaginable.

More than kind, at times so greatly
more than he deserves.

A CERTAIN APTITUDE,
Or
LACK THEREOF

Playing the Koto

The koto has a magic of its own.
I tried to play one in Okinawa as a young Marine
where two G.I.s harassed an old woman who claimed
to be the koto Master of Okinawa and Japan.

As a boxer with the build of an oak tree,
I sent the young G.I.s scurrying. So the koto
Master asked me if I'd like to learn to play.
"Sure would," I said, and the lesson began

with her playing the airiest tune I'd ever heard.
Then she placed my fingers on the long strands
of strings and softly plucked a chord or two
with her hands guiding me.

"You try," she said. On my own, the strings stung the air
like mad bees, like someone had whacked their hornets' nest.
Again, she guided my fingers, and when she released
her hands from mine, the hornets were madder

than before, but I kept on, until she put up the palm
of her hand to beckon me to what was surely a sign
to rest, when she gently whispered,
"You will never learn to play the koto."

A Man in Beggar Rags

A man in beggar rags approached me
and asked who I "am."

"I am Jonathan," I said.
"No," he replied, "I asked who you are."

So philosophical. Caught me off guard
that a man in shambles seemed

to be interested in me, existentially.
I went on about being an Independent,

but leaning toward Democrat. I spent
much of my childhood in West Virginia

and came to be known as a Naturalist.
And though I am not sectarian of faith,

I believe in some form of God. And
on it went, standing outside the Eugene

Oregon Mission where he listened
carefully, and finally said, "What

I meant was, are you in line for chow,
or do you work here?"

*Tony Abbott loved this poem. He laughed when I read it
and said, "That ending really caught me off guard!" For all
the downtrodden poems I wrote for his classes, I'm glad I
finally wrote something that made him laugh.*

When I was in Eugene, Oregon for the University of Oregon's MFA program in 1982, I often had lunch with an out-of-work chef who offered his perspective on Easterners.

"People from the East are often too high on themselves," he would say, more than once.

After writing the poem, it didn't take long for me to realize the out-of-work chef was probably right.

I used to give him money to supplement a very small stipend he received from the state government, which was about to run out, and the Eugene Oregon Mission, which fed people who often circled the mission during mealtime. Georgia Pacific had pulled out; interest rates were going through the roof. It was similar to everything I had seen on TV and read about comparing this to Eugene's Great Depression.

I wrote this poem based on my experience with the out-of-work chef, and the downtrodden at the Eugene mission, regarding those waiting for a meal.

AFTERWORD
(When Near the End …)

Fallen Petals

At seventy-five, life has become full of goodbyes.
And all those good folks who lived on the riverbanks
are gone, leaving me to live life on concrete among
signs of do's and don'ts.

It is to remind us: we are the childlike elderly.

No dragonflies, few butterflies, only here I roost
with the pigeons and crows.

My wife asks, "Where are the flowerbeds I so dearly loved?"
Our simpler world is filled with identifying bird calls and
drowning bad memories, unhappy thoughts.

It is an old man's prerogative to find simple joys where
he can, cherish the little pleasures that surprise him
now and then.

Even as the redbuds come back again.

*In April, 2023, we moved into a retirement community. In the first
two months, four people in our building passed away. Gurneys
have a way of awakening those who are left from the dead.*

The Heart Knows Who We Are

The heart knows who we are
　　　with all the hoopla in the world,
among the love and hate,
care and those who do not care.

When wisdom calls, it is the heart
　　　that answers, regardless of politics,
religion, or what the mind wants to believe.

The most beautiful scene I'd ever seen—
　　　the pink moss waterfall, the three-color
sky beyond, purple, pink and orange.

I felt mindless then. It did not matter what I thought.
　　　I did not know who I was just then.
It did not matter, only that I did not want this moment

to disappear. I wanted my father to see this scene,
　　　but he had passed. I wanted my mother to see
this scene. But she, too, had passed.

Alone, the heart has new wishes, wishes that it
　　　had time for who those it loved, now gone.
It wishes I had known better then.

A Certain Grace

The grass learns by heart to grow, as do
the dandelions, each a distance apart
to allow the other to breathe.

There is a certain grace there on display.
The sun lathers them in dew, primed for a mower's
aim. The blade scrapes their tender skin.

Near half the size they used to be, they wait
for new dew, the elixir that restores their former
selves, without lament for who they once were.

A Child and Parents' Wilderness

There were no familiar places
in my dreams or reality,
only delusions of what
could have been.

There was only a wilderness
of bitterness and rage,
doubts and passions too
intense for one child to bear.

The uninvited guest, darkness,
came in shapes of shadows
surrounding my bedroom door.
Outside that room, a cacophony

of contempt burst about, fading
only to return, the sweet sickness
of love and hate, hourly exposed.
There were no flowers in my

dreams, only thorns. I was
in the company of strangers,
parents, I would never come
to know. Their passion was

mainly between the two of them.
I would sojourn, relative
to relative. And when grown,
fade into that same wilderness

of bitterness and rage. An old
man now, I can find flowers
everywhere among those thorns.
It took nearly a lifetime to do.

Tiny Eternities

In the quiet, we can still hear who we are,
we who come to Earth on loan. Morning

by morning, we live in our tiny eternities,
one day at a time. It is a debt we pay

with a fervent gaze of moments when joy
overcomes the anger and fear that once

was. I have loved best how tiny eternities
unfold, one by one, none so worthy of my

existence than another. Out of the daring
darkness, violence of my youth, I have come

to find love in this world. All that rises and
opens in spring. Serene, wordless harmony.

It is a lesson the universe sends us. No more
a stranger to what it airs.

Recent Hospital Stay
(July 17, 2023)

In my recent hospital stay, I was told
I have white matter disease, three years
remaining to accomplish what I will.

I search for words that used to come
so easily. (What is a poet without words?)

Like a rusted engine that sputters, yet
still gathers steam before it's over,
time to time.

But, oh, the energy it takes!
Sputter on, dear engine, sputter on!

Once believed a self-made man, I have
come to believe in none of it. Tossed
seven diplomas in a storage bin, and
said, "There, that's where you belong!"

What intimidates me now are those
who expect too much of me in what
may be near my final days (and me
of myself).

The shadowy images of my mind
of another time when I cherished words—
they magnetized me—stuck to a tongue,
then so fluidly disengaged.

At times, so tart, at times sweet, or
like the waterfalls that poured into
a rhythm on a page.

Nothing stranger than losing all that.

Nothing.

Acknowledgments

I took non-credit "senior citizen" poetry classes under Tony Abbott who near his passing was entered into the North Carolina Literary Hall of Fame. And I give credit to those senior citizen poets as well. We met monthly between 2018–2021.

But without Barbara, there would have been no Tony Abbott or senior citizen poets in my life. I suspect I would have given up writing poetry long before that.

About the Author

Jonathan Ian Elliott has taken a number of non-credit courses under Tony Abbott and received a Second Place finish and an Honorary Mention as an emerging poet in West Virginia Writers Group's Spring 2017 and 2020 contests, respectively.

He published several poems in Virginia Commonwealth University's literary magazine, an article in *The Richmond Times-Dispatch* on hitchhiking as a student, as well as publishing in *Bitterroot*, a New York poetry publication in 1972.

He taught English composition at Purdue University as a graduate student in 1972–73, attended the University of Oregon's MFA program in 1982, and published an essay in *Dance to the Music of Story*, edited by David Boje, Professor at New Mexico State University, in 2010.

www.ingramcontent.com/pod-product-compliance
Lightning Source LLC
LaVergne TN
LVHW041200080426
835511LV00006B/685